Barclay Butera

Getaways and Retreats

BARCLAY BUTERA
GETAWAYS AND RETREATS

PHOTOGRAPHY BY MARK LOHMAN

GIBBS SMITH
TO ENRICH AND INSPIRE HUMANKIND

DEDICATION

My passion for interior design took hold when I became the new business development associate for my mother, Karen Butera, who runs a highly regarded interior design firm. Working alongside her on her various projects, I soon realized that her exceptional level of taste and attention to detail was the key to her incredible success. The experience and training I received during those years was the most priceless education one could get. She taught me about the art of symmetry, combining colors and layering textures with patterns, but most of all she instilled in me a work ethic of honesty, dedication and perseverance. Watching her attain every goal that she set for herself gave me the drive and motivation to succeed in becoming who I am today. I express my heartfelt appreciation and gratitude for changing the course of my life and for the tremendous role she has played in my professional endeavors. Mom, this book is dedicated to you with love.

CONTENTS

Introduction   9

INTRODUCTION

When all is said and done, the vast majority of our lives are spent within a very narrow region of the map: our borough, our neighborhood, our zip code, our side of town. As a result, we can't help but become creatures of habit, developing daily routines from which we rarely stray. We find ourselves shopping at the same local markets, frequenting the same quaint coffee shops and dining at the same handful of restaurants. We really get to know all the charming little nooks and crannies of our hometowns, and it is in these places that our fondest memories are made.

For the most part, I find comfort in this consistency and even revel in it; but at the onset of each season, I feel myself craving a change of scenery, an escape to break up the monotony and push my inner reset button. The only remedy for this hankering to realign my state of mind is to take a vacation; to retreat to a place where I can exchange the familiar for something unique and unknown.

I am a person who delights in all seasons: the timeless serenity of summer, the stimulating preparedness and crisp wistfulness of autumn, the hasty and robust outset of spring, as well as the peculiar industriousness and oddly bipolar indoor/outdoor exhilaration of winter. I have found that I seek out retreats that both soothe and invigorate me, depending on the season. Retreats transport me back to fond passages of my life or forward to long-anticipated chapters of contentment.

When I was a child, my vacations were primarily dictated by the three-month breaks between school years and were always synonymous with summer, water and sun. We would travel as a family to the coasts and shorelines of various tropical locales, and I would soak up every moment of the day playing in the saltwater and basking on the sandy beaches. This is where my true love of everything nautical began. As a teenager, I developed a great passion for skiing and was lucky enough to make the trek to several picturesque mountain resorts during the winter breaks of my high school years. The smell of fresh pine and feel of the crisp mountain air on my face as I raced down the slopes gave me a genuine appreciation for the great outdoors. My college days brought opportunities to study abroad in several countries, where I was influenced by the astonishing beauty of other cultures and their unique treasures. It was on these retreats and getaways that my eyes were opened to a new way of seeing things, and even today, I continue to draw on these experiences for inspiration in my designs.

Whether our escape is to a tranquil desert spa, rustic mountain lodge, scenic seaside resort or picturesque villa, we all have our own version of the perfect getaway, and we all feel the same sense of anticipation as the day of departure to our chosen landscape approaches. But no matter how wonderful our vacation is, the thirst for comfort takes over and we find ourselves eager to return to the familiarity of home. Once there, we can instill in our surroundings a look and feel that will saturate us with that which we have sought out: the icy blue and silver landscape of winter; the rusts and shimmering golds from the burnished woods of fall; the exhilarating and colorful rejuvenation of spring; and the uncluttered nautical culture of summer. Seasons will always bring change, and the places we go and the experiences we take part in will continue to influence and shape our lives.

SPRING

Overstatement aside, spring is all about rebirth and rejuvenation. From the initial budding blossoms of the cherry trees to the first crocuses bursting from hardened soil, the world is coming alive once again in a celebration of new beginnings. Whatever one's age—and I mean this—getting through the cold, bleak winter and enjoying the privilege of witnessing the miracle of spring takes years off your life. Seeing the world come into bloom once more, one can't help but feel the desire to hope, plan and dream again. The winter landscape of charcoal, graphite, amber and grey is shattered into oblivion by the arrival of color in the form of vibrant greens, bold reds, dazzling purples and brilliant blues. Bare shoulders are exposed and open-toed shoes make their way back onto the scene. It is impossible for spring to not evoke the blissful sensation of awakening to the sudden concerto of light and color and space— and eternal possibility.

The arrival of spring packs a mighty punch to the senses; the contrast of the vivid blue sky against the bright white clouds, the lovely scent of flowering gardenias and star jasmine, the prickly sensation of freshly cut grass between your toes, the merry ballads of the birds out and about chirping once again. In response, I like to expand my spring palette with various tones of cream and ivory, celadon and happy shades of beige. And always spots of color, riotous color wherever a dark corner exists. These rooms don't need overcrowding with rugs and occasional tables and tabletop accessories; in fact they suffer from it. There needs to be space for growth and expansion and culmination. The naked floors and newly opened doors collaborate with light colors to make movement—any movement—that much easier and more playful.

The arrival of spring is truly a license to edit, purge and streamline. You've got all summer to luxuriate in constancy and comfort; so, for now, stop where you are and take notice of the drama unfolding everywhere around you. Lean into your life again and be a part of the pulsating beat of spring.

FACING: A palette of serene neutrals punctuated with crisp blue and white accents set the stage for a sunlit spring retreat. Ivory molding unifies living and dining areas of the open floor plan.

ABOVE: Here, a cane-backed bench creates just enough delineation for an intimate dining setting.

LEFT: Diamond-paned glass cabinets and a white marble backsplash keep the mood radiant and refined in the small adjoining bar area.

ABOVE: A vintage sideboard anchors the entry hall. Oversized pottery vessels and wicker baskets bring earthy appeal to a graceful setting.

FACING: Upholstered dining chairs with short box-pleated skirts further the tailored aesthetic of the retreat. A cane-backed bamboo bar stool allows for conversation with the cook.

The restrained palette of sand and cream beautifully sets off blue and white accents in the master suite.

LEFT: Passionate red walls and sleek accessories underscore classic Hollywood glamour in this striking urban retreat. The chair, upholstered in plum velvet, is a decadent indulgence.

FACING: Plush textures and animal prints collaborate to create a glamorously inviting room. Eclectic accent pillows adorn a tufted chesterfield-style sofa.

FACING: In the dining room, a shaded chandelier hangs over a double-pedestal dining table and a suite of dining chairs covered in leopard-print fabric. French doors lead to a terrace enveloped by stands of bamboo and blooming bougainvillea.

ABOVE LEFT: Simple gilded bookcases play a supporting role, lending a note of informality to the dining space.

ABOVE: Decorative objects, mementos, and books collected over time are integrated on an étagère, mixing function with playfulness.

LEFT: A framed portrait of Paul Newman imbues the stunning space with more than a hint of old Hollywood style and charm.

ABOVE: A hallway functions as a gallery space for prized prints from the owner's photography collection.

FACING: The master bedroom, rich in leopard print and neutral hues of cream and chocolate, is designed to serve as a revitalizing personal space.

ℬ Hazel Drive

ABOVE: In the living room, a pair of Barclay Butera Home leather Regency chairs flanks a vintage Louis Vuitton trunk, while stenciled giraffe-hide pillows add a jolt of pattern.

RIGHT: A custom armoire serves as a handsome focal point for a living room that celebrates the fusion of traditional furnishings with clean, upbeat style.

FACING: Detailing with starfish, sinuous curves, and glass elaborate on the light and airy theme for spring.

ABOVE: The broad blue-and-white stripe of a Barclay Butera Home skirted Hampton chair delivers a vivacious visual punch to an otherwise overlooked corner.

ABOVE: Designed for cooking and entertaining, the professionally appointed kitchen reflects clean, streamlined styling.

LEFT: Function and style combine in polished nickel fixtures, surfaces, and chunky hardware. Dark wood finishes keep it traditional.

FACING: Low-back barstools and a bistro bar table create a delightfully impromptu cafe moment for a quick bite or lingering latte.

FACING: A guest bedroom presents a timeless color scheme that mixes subtle tones with bright patterned accents.

ABOVE: This luxuriously comfortable master bedroom is the ultimate place to find rest.

LEFT: Identical pedestal basins, mounted oval mirrors, and chandeliers nestled in twin niches allow for individual domains in the master bath.

PREVIOUS OVERLEAF: The casual elegance of spring continues in the dining room, where each element exudes a graceful note.

LEFT: Grasscloth-covered walls and a sisal rug invite tactile interest in a family room. A leather Sussex sectional sofa by Barclay Butera Home provides ample seating for family and friends. Blue-centric pillows pepper the palette with shots of crisp, bold color.

ABOVE: An oar mounted over the flat-screen television and shell accents are nods to the coastal setting. Ottomans covered in soft blue linen are tucked comfortably under the set.

FACING: A European-style stone fountain inset in a stone wall transforms an outdoor terrace with soothing splashing sounds and a timeless, classic look.

ABOVE: A spacious roof deck overlooks a coastal setting. The cushioned outdoor furnishings are kept simple so as not to compete with the view.

LEFT: Table and chairs center a covered outdoor living space. Bright white latticework adds character and charm, while a built-in fireplace permits year-round enjoyment.

Glenoak Avenue

ABOVE: A pastel palette is an ideal foundation for the elegant layering of elements. Pillows in subtle tones with playful patterns accent the space, adding softness and a lovely touch of spring.

RIGHT: A pair of chairs covered in refined pale pink act as graceful cohorts for a delicate bar table. Floral prints ensure that the spring mood will be in bloom all year long.

FACING: Glam textures and shapes punctuate the overall soothing tone of the residence.

ABOVE: Serene green wallpaper creates an ethereal spring ambiance. Pink hues accent the grouping; a sunburst mirror provides the crowning touch.

Silver and brilliant blue tones partner in a visual symphony
inspired by the icy chill of winter.

SUMMER

Summertime. To a great many, this is the most anticipated of the seasons and the quintessential period to get away. We long for it in the dead of winter and it rarely disappoints. Long, lazy days spent outside and warm nights are aplenty. Back doors are left open more often than they are closed and scheduled routines are nonexistent. There seems to be time enough for everything and everyone and then some.

And that is why I strive for literal timelessness with regard to the design and installation of summer-centric retreats. Heavy drapery is dispatched in favor of sheer gauzes, semitransparent roman shades or blinds of bamboo. Darkly stained hardwoods on floors and furnishings are eschewed in favor of pine and blonde woods along with the simpler, less solid and more easily moved rattans and wickers. I also like to minimize the sharp distinction between indoors and outdoors and maximize the likelihood of impromptu al fresco entertaining. There is plenty of room for corals and sea fans and collected shells. Beach glass and maritime artifacts are among the ample seating and carefree tabletops I like to employ around these rooms. Soft laundered linens, crisp cottons and colorful nautical flags really celebrate this relaxed approach to the dog days of summer, where the goal is one of unbroken comfort without the need for a beginning or an end.

Summer encompasses a stretch of idle days that are appreciated in the moment and savored at lights out. The hallmark of this time of year is the classic summer holiday, the Fourth of July, a day that serves to punch up the steady stream of rest and relaxation and that highlights the exuberance and excitement of the season. The strident reds, virtuous whites and Americana blues are consistently woven into my designs to underscore the hard-won delights of summer. And after a day on the water or the back nine and before the afternoon barbecues begin, the timelessness of our own independence is never more evident.

LEFT: A clean palette and uncluttered lines result in easy elegance for this summer retreat. On a Barclay Butera Bel Air coffee table, a sculptural ceramic vase and organic coral fragment provide a decorative moment of contrast. Grey walls allow the art to pop.

ABOVE: A counter separates a galley kitchen from a comfy sitting area in this flow-through beach getaway.

RIGHT: A rich color scheme of cream, café au lait and cocoa allows the progression of spaces to seamlessly play together. Framed shell lithographs cheerfully animate wall space.

BELOW: The bamboo canopy bed feels luxurious and casual at the same time. Decorative pillows in caramel velvet, patterned tapestry fabric and supple leather add to the coziness and ease of the space.

The colors of sand and sea steer the decor in this light-filled guest bedroom. Organic coral motifs and blue-and-white chinoiserie accent lamps collaborate to enliven the pretty palette.

Tones of turquoise, teal and terra-cotta team up in this bold, eye-catching bedroom. The Moroccan-inspired bedspread provides a graphic dose of pattern.

FACING: Stylishly deployed, an arrangement of artwork and accessory creates a sophisticated summer vignette.

ABOVE: Set on an elevation overlooking a harbor, a deck frames the view with classic furnishings and nautical details.

LEFT: An open shelving tower in a master bath easily handles stacks of towels and keeps robes within easy reach.

LEFT: This charming beach cottage is embellished with a network of terraces and al fresco rooms that celebrate the indoor-outdoor lifestyle of summer.

FACING: A brick staircase climbs a landscaped cliff to a shingled summer getaway painted light blue to blend in to the beach palette. Large terra-cotta pots brimming with seasonal flowering plants soften the angles of the steep pathway.

ABOVE: Custom floor-to-ceiling beadboard walls in pale pistachio make this beach house living room informal and intimate. The recessed bookcase behind the Barclay Butera Stratford sofa displays beachcombing relics. A mirrored cathedral window fits perfectly in the wall space between doorways.

FACING: The room contains many decorative touches, including starfish and seashells used as bottle stoppers and an antique silver vase foaming with fresh-cut hydrangeas.

FACING: Employing crisp white wainscoting and sleek upholstered dining chairs gives this small space added dimension. The bamboo window shade allows for just the right amount of sunlight to wash over the nook.

ABOVE: A small potted palm presides over a summertime tablescape.

RIGHT: The custom bedding with floral motif brings the outdoors right inside. French doors open onto a private side courtyard.

BELOW: A bed dominates a small guest room, but the white duvet with a simple navy embroidered border keeps the overall impression neat and uncluttered.

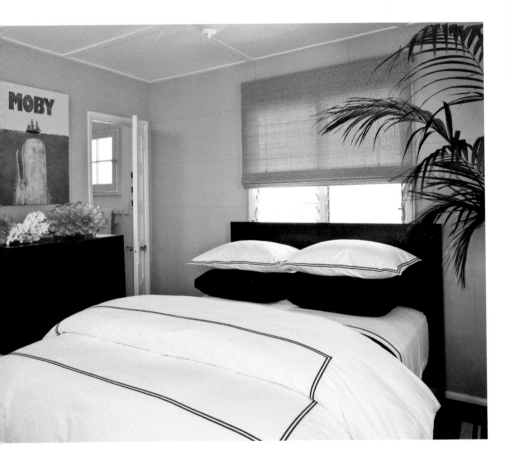

FACING: A handsome ocean-side deck is furnished with classic picnic table and benches painted sailcloth white. Pillows clad in solid and playful argyle fabric introduce a splash of green into the scenery.

ABOVE: Distressed signage promotes the vintage allure of this shingled beach house.

ABOVE: Brightly colored Adirondack chairs, hydrangeas in bloom and the American flag epitomize summer at its peak.

FACING: An upper balcony and roof deck trimmed in railing, a lighthouse turret, and a porthole window imbue this quaint beachside summer house with nautical quirkiness.

LEFT ABOVE: A built-in bookcase with beadboard backing painted red makes a cheery backdrop for a display of maritime treasures. In the foreground, Paris club chairs from Barclay Butera Home in custom two-tone upholstery and flag-red pillows supply additional snap.

FACING BELOW: A miniature sailboat hull brimming with starfish and sand dollars keeps the beachy spirit in play on the coffee table.

ABOVE: A patriotic red, white, and blue color scheme drenches the living room. The bold stripes of the Barclay Butera Home Hampton sectional sofa ensure that the festive spirit will not be limited to just one July day.

ABOVE: Layered Barclay Butera Home throw pillows accent the sofa. Custom-painted coffered ceiling adds visual interest and delineates the living room space from the dining room.

LEFT: The stars and stripes aesthetic extends to serving pieces and glassware.

FACING: Bold navy-and-white-stripe rug, vintage pine hutch, blue-and-white china, and iron chandelier put an Americana spin on this casual, classically styled dining room.

FACING: While this cozy kitchen is grounded in traditional style, the mix of finishes, from polished marble to gleaming nickel, gives it a modern vibe. In the foreground, a cushion with a nautical rigging motif echoes the home's red, white and blue color scheme.

ABOVE: A narrow passageway space is converted into a cheerful work and storage space with white cabinets and beautiful hardwood floors. The bench is a great place to kick off your topsiders.

LEFT: In this powder room, blue-and-white wallpaper of sailing yacht schematics adds graphic energy to a compact space. Round mirror and window evoke a ship's portholes.

RIGHT: A custom Aegean-blue bedspread (and matching dog bed) patterned with whimsical seashore illustrations is flanked by vintage rattan side tables. Captain's wheel lamps keep the room shipshape. The adorable white poodle ties the whole look together.

BELOW: A luxurious, light-filled master bath pays homage to the beach environment with oversized coral fragments, conch shells and starfish. The minimal sand-and-white palette gives the room an elegant and relaxed feeling.

ABOVE: This vivacious bunk room was designed to accommodate as many as six young house guests. Bold red-and-white stripes and checks, porthole windows, and a vaulted ceiling festooned with nautical flags deliver maximum maritime impact.

FACING ABOVE: Beige carpeting is durable and suggests a sandy beach just a stone's throw away from this vacation home. Crisp white molding and ocean blue walls are quintessentially coastal.

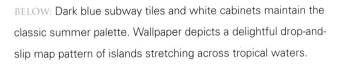

BELOW: Dark blue subway tiles and white cabinets maintain the classic summer palette. Wallpaper depicts a delightful drop-and-slip map pattern of islands stretching across tropical waters.

FACING: All manner of seashore artifacts enhance the experience of a summer holiday at the beach.

ABOVE: A clamshell fountain crowns this outdoor living space, which features open-work metal furnishings cushioned in classic navy fabric with white piping. The area is sheltered by an expansive striped canopy.

FACING: Jewel tones of turquoise and topaz are layered to provide a vibrant effect in this urban retreat. Eccentric furnishings and decorative objects collaborate in a visual feast inspired by exotic destinations.

BELOW: Gold-leaf ceiling, tufted velvet wingback chairs, and damask-patterned wall covering conspire to transform the space into a dramatic stage.

FACING: Classic white woodwork and porcelain pedestal sink mesh effortlessly with an ornate mirror, Moroccan sconces, and idiosyncratic bottle-bottom window.

ABOVE: An elegant white marble console with a dramatic silhouette serves as a focal point in this stunning niche. A Moroccan pendant lamp lends an air of mystery.

LEFT: The timeless pairing of black and white has long epitomized refinement and sophistication. Here, a black lacquered dining table and white modern molded chairs offer visual punch without relying on layers of pattern.

FACING: This dynamic bedroom interior artfully mixes saturated colors at their boldest and fabrics at their most sumptuous.

RIGHT: A city view serves as a focal point for a space rich in red, reflective surfaces, and animal prints.

BELOW: The zebra console table and cinnabar-hued walls instill this retreat with a sense of exotic elegance. Stark white leather cubes can be recruited for additional seating.

LEFT: The vision for this bedroom was to create a contemporary yet romantic atmosphere inspired by exquisite, luxurious fabrics and saturated, muscular tones of chocolate, bronze and navy.

ABOVE: An abstract painting in luscious blues hangs above a knockout mid-century cabinet.

AUTUMN

The onset of autumn marks a time for vacations to end and everyday routines to resume. Flip-flops and bathing suits are stashed away in exchange for cozy sweaters and button-down oxfords. Balmy beach days are replaced with twilight porch parties and Saturday tailgates, and the early dusks only punctuate our inevitable shift toward dormancy. There is a cliché about fall being a time to take stock and make a sober survey of the milestones and regrets of one's life. While this is a bit too heavy-handed for me, the pivot from the exuberance of summer to the hibernation of winter does provoke me to reflect on the fact that seasons pass all too quickly and that time is a fleeting thing I must never take for granted.

Like the smell of a crackling fire or the sound of rain hitting the pavement, autumn has a warm and soothing effect on my senses. The cool, crisp air, falling foliage, dampening earth, and long, dark nights tend to shift my design aesthetic to one of lusty earth tones, deep ambers and velvety grey-browns. These palettes are then punctuated with dusty goldenrods, striking crimsons and bold tangerines.

I find that the odd contrast between the pre-winter and post-summer days that alternate in fall is a license for me to revel in visual contrast. I like to use more white than many would think prudent after Labor Day, pairing it with animal prints and creating an intermixture with textured upholstery fabrics: a bronze silk on white jacquard or an oyster linen mixed with espresso wool. I think paisley is a two-point conversion for the fall sitting room, with its strangely sinuous and luxuriant foliage rendered in browns, reds and yellows. Rich leather in caramel and chocolate tones provides an excellent accent to the more intricate elements in the decor.

While it is impossible to fix or freeze this season, I find that by showcasing bold colors, vibrant textures, and opulent jewel tones, I can capture nature's beauty, infuse a satisfying and nostalgic feeling of the fall season, and leave one always wanting more.

Perched on a hillside, an expansive mountain retreat dressed up with stone facade and railroad
ties pays homage to its western roots and offers the promise of rest and relaxation.

FACING: The great room, featuring a soaring ceiling and magnificent antler chandelier, is decorated in soothing textured neutrals.

ABOVE: Against a putty-colored wall, a whimsical painting of a cowboy in chaps and duster coat becomes a focal point behind a Barclay Butera Home Paxton sofa.

ABOVE: Collected objects reflect the home's proximity to nature.

FACING: There are just enough texture and color in the space to establish presence, but not so much as to compete with the views or the client's vast collection of Western art.

ABOVE: Elegant but understated decor allows the gorgeous view to take center stage in the dining room. The overscaled houndstooth pattern of the Barclay Butera Home Lido host chair brings a touch of panache.

FACING ABOVE: Hurricane lamps provide gleam, while bighorn candle holders emphasize the locale.

BELOW: Cleverly wired from within, natural-looking faux candles on an iron fixture cast a warm, flattering glow over dinner-time proceedings.

FACING: Nineteenth-century-inspired custom furniture and a palette of muted tans and greens create a laid-back and restful bedroom vignette.

ABOVE: Natural materials lend this powder room a rustic air. A butler's pantry adjacent to the kitchen boasts a built-in plate rack as a signature feature.

ABOVE: A vintage wagon wheel, an antique rocker, a stag sculpture, and a Labrador retriever are just a few of the exterior components that maintain the overall rustic vibe of the estate.

FACING: An intimate and cozy setting for al fresco entertaining embodies the spirit of relaxed country living.

LEFT: Varied rooflines, along with the stone and wood facade, articulate the expansiveness of this ravishing mountain retreat.

ABOVE: The stylistic contrast of a formal Louis-style bergère chair with casual weathered floors and fieldstone walls creates a quaint and disarming entry hall moment.

FACING: The exposed timbers, extreme heights, and large windows imbue this living room environment with enormous stature. Chocolate brown Paxton sofas by Barclay Butera Home bring the space down to earth and keep the color scheme seasonal.

ABOVE: To make the momentous room feel inviting and intimate, a grouping of Manhattan chairs by Barclay Butera Home creates an atypical sitting area around a modern, muscular cocktail table. Horn details and animal prints add a real swagger to the place.

RIGHT: Colorful and contemporary abstract paintings create a feeling of juxtaposition in this otherwise rustic mountain retreat. These woven-back chairs have a handcrafted look and play off the outdoor elements just beyond the window frame.

BELOW: In keeping with the home's aesthetic of rural sophistication, the dining room is furnished with a long antique table and an iron light fixture with strong, modern lines.

LEFT: Generously sized upholstered Sahara barstools from Barclay Butera Home provide counter seating for quick meals at the marble-top island. Nearby, a large window invites turning foliage of autumn into the kitchen.

ABOVE: The mix of wood finishes and rich materials gives this kitchen dining area a traditional look with an opulent twist.

A subtle palette is used to create a cohesive, welcoming space in this master suite private escape. The Barclay Butera Home Beverly sofa is the perfect place to curl up and forget about the chill outside.

ABOVE: Aesthetic lines and natural wood pieces create a fun and inviting game room in a mountain retreat.

LEFT: Natural elements play a key role in this family room. A sectional sofa makes room for a pair of Barclay Butera Home Soho cubes.

RIGHT: Plush leather Manhattan sectional sofa by Barclay Butera Home, exposed beams, and expressionistic lighting deliver a design that is the very definition of masculine chic: luxurious, warm, earthy, and extremely comfortable.

ABOVE: A wall of windows in this enclave flaunts the natural beauty of the landscape.

LEFT: A narrow hallway becomes a functional mudroom, with pegs for hanging coats and a bench for pulling off muddy wellies. A map of America fashioned out of vintage license plates can be glimpsed through a doorway.

BELOW: The mountain setting plays in to this bedroom design, but not with obvious motifs. The warm, autumnal palette mimics the beauty of nature through the window.

FACING: Vintage luggage, shimmering hurricane lamps, and a couple of knockout lamps round out the room with texture, scale and style.

LEFT: In the living area, armchairs covered in cream fabric act as an endnote to a conversation area anchored by a large square coffee table. The relaxed but refined grouping includes two streamlined Harbor sofas and Claire storage ottomans, both from Barclay Butera Home.

ABOVE: An antique sterling silver tea service and spray of orchids add quintessential strokes of elegance.

The sinuous shapes of the iron sconces climbing the stairwell mimic the graceful lines of the staircase, which curves off the entry hall.

An iron chandelier with a dramatic silhouette serves as a focal point for this casually elegant dining room. The large-scale host and hostess chairs in oyster linen offer a seamless punctuation to the perfectly symmetrical space.

LEFT: Expansive stretches of cream cabinets coupled with a white tile backsplash give this kitchen a clean, crisp, and spacious presence. Upholstered stools at the island provide a comfortable perch for coffee and conversation any time of the day.

ABOVE: Muted blues, uncluttered lines, and vaulted ceiling create an airy ambience in this refreshing master suite overlooking a harbor.

LEFT: The fantastic light, the views, and the seasonal colors work together to epitomize rustic sophistication in its most appealing state.

FACING: This warm, inviting space encompasses beautiful structure, impeccable balance, and classical elegance.

ABOVE: The sculptural iron chandelier adds the finishing touch to the mix of upholstered chairs and built-in banquette, making the dining room both informal and inviting.

FACING ABOVE: Blue-and-white porcelain ginger jars flanking a dramatic orchid arrangement are the perfect accessories to top this sunburst entry piece.

BELOW: Carefully selected fabrics impart the colors of an iconic autumnal palette to this living room vignette.

FACING: A color scheme consisting primarily of neutrals needs small doses of color to enliven the space. Here, pillows with lively patterns, a striped rug, and silk lampshades accent the room, adding punctuations of turquoise, red, and blue.

ABOVE: In this effortlessly stunning kitchen, the polished marble countertops and backsplash help to offset the hardwood floors and cabinetry.

LEFT: Finely crafted furnishings, unique fabrics, and dramatic lighting were carefully chosen to bring style and sophistication to this dining room without sacrificing comfort or rustic appeal.

LEFT: This assortment of cozy sofas and chairs in inviting monochromatic fabrications creates the pampering atmosphere of a relaxing lodge.

BELOW: A handsome built-in unit keeps all the electronic entertainment hardware completely out of view.

Mark Lohman 2007

ABOVE: A pair of Barclay Butera Home Carmel lounge chairs upholstered in animal print flank a chest of drawers crowned with topiary.

FACING BELOW: Mirrors with rough-hewn frames continue the distressed, woodsy flair of the home.

ABOVE: A bedroom swathed in autumnal hues is a mandatory element in every mountain retreat. The custom bedding layers organic textures and warm hues, providing a cozy and inviting effect.

LEFT: The Barclay Butera Home leather Regency chairs articulated around his tufted and upholstered Elizabeth ottoman create a warm space rich with classic elegance. The Greek key nailhead detail around the base of the ottoman provides a touch of the unexpected.

ABOVE: Gorgeous pedestal tables against a built-in banquette replicate arrangements typical of reading libraries at grand estates.

RIGHT: This picture-perfect living space reflects a blend of both haute style and comfort. The vivid color of the landscape paintings stands out against the neutral palette and subtle textures of the upholstery and wallcovering. Matching porcelain lamps on side tables flank the tufted Greystone sofa by Barclay Butera Home.

BELOW: Thoughtful accents can catapult a room from merely appealing to triumphant. This strikingly beautiful desk is adorned with personal mementos and carefully considered decorative accessories.

GREYSTONE ESTATE ❖ 153

WINTER

With its stripped-down landscapes and withdrawn aesthetics, winter is paradoxically the most mysterious of seasons. Familiar views are transformed into a myriad of silvery greys and darkened beiges; trees are rendered into skeletal charcoal drawings; sweeps of hillsides are simplified and obscured by accumulated snow. Individuals particularly drawn to winter—and I'm one of them—find these dismal environments intriguing, refreshing and visually dramatic.

With regard to interior design of winter vacation retreats, I rely first and foremost on simple common sense born of necessity and embellished by history and tradition. Thicker fabrics used throughout the house—heavy linens, velvet window treatments and overstuffed upholstery—are a necessity to create a warm and inviting environment. I also love to incorporate a variety of leather pieces, animal hides and antlers for similar reasons: they not only blunt the chill of walls and floors but serve to bring the life of the winter wilderness indoors.

The traditional holiday pairing of crimson and evergreen are always welcome, as they look great by firelight and cue the moods and festivities of hot toddy and tea drinkers year-round. I also like to incorporate the visual fullness of plaid, as it tends to claim space definitively and creates a reassuring sense of enclosure and coziness. Rooms painted in icy tones of blue evoke the European glamour of winter hot spots Scandinavia and St. Petersburg.

Of course, no wonderland is complete without fabulous touches of visual whimsy and fun artifacts that serve to punch up a space—think vintage winter sportswear, distressed signage, provisioning gear, coat racks and foundling mittens, all of which revisit the theme that life in the winter is hard but also breathtaking. Basically, anything natural or man-made that finds its way into a toasty winter getaway has earned its keep—and maybe even pride of place on a mantel.

LEFT: A large-scale sofa faces off with a pair of lounge chairs in a relaxed open space, effortlessly evoking the feel of a luxe lodge. Strokes of red, featured in both the traditional tartan fabric of the adjoining dining area and the upholstery of Barclay Butera Home Somerset chairs, tie the two spaces together.

BELOW: An exposed staircase with wood railings further conveys the sense of openness.

FACING: Two imposing iron light fixtures drop from magnificent timbers that are holding up the structure. The warm, inviting ski lodge vibe inside almost supersedes any incentive to venture outside and hit the slopes.

ABOVE: Rich meets rustic in this handsome leather armchair with oversized nailhead trim.

ABOVE: The home's den boasts a theme of rugged luxury with a distressed leather sofa and a couple of chunky woven lounge chairs.

FACING ABOVE: A pair of horn accessories and a lantern light fixture enhance the cabin's cozy ambiance.

BELOW: Every element exudes graceful charm: the antique chest, organic wood lamp bases, an array of blue-and-white porcelain.

RIGHT: Inviting colors and delightful patterns distinguish this comfortable guest bedroom. An inviting leather chair in the corner provides the perfect place to curl up with a book and a blanket.

BELOW: Barclay Butera Home Wyland chairs and Sussex sofa are grouped around an antique wood steamer trunk in the master suite.

Elemental and intimate, the master bedroom uses anchor pieces like a grand canopy bed, horn and cowhide chair, and, of course, an alluring fireplace to embody the theme of chalet chic.

The master bathroom is composed of two distinct areas: the vanity on one side and basin with built-in cabinets on the other.

ABOVE: Warm, textured neutrals team up to create a pleasant cabin-like bedroom refuge.

FACING: This small room celebrates the traditional rustic furnishings: a horned mirror, a chest dressed in cowhide, and a supple leather camp chair.

ABOVE: Winter is ever present in dramatic expanses of glass, wood and stone. A sophisticated palette of neutrals keeps the look elegant and earthy.

FACING: A Barclay Butera Home Manhattan sectional embraces the rustic coffee table. Natural materials warm up the extreme heights and large windows.

ABOVE: Wildlife-inspired accessories deftly add touches of whimsy to the environment.

FACING: Expansive windows connect this dining room's interior to its glorious exterior, giving a constant reminder of the beauty just outside. Feed sack dining chairs are a nod to the relaxed environment.

FACING: A roomy kitchen facing the living area is designed for great cooking and entertaining. A center island and two banks of windows lend a sense of symmetry to the area.

ABOVE: The Barclay Butera Home Townley console and a pair of Claire storage ottomans work in concert to enliven a transition zone. Framed tree etchings and artfully arranged vintage snowshoes animate the expansive wall divider.

FACING: The ski lodge theme continues in a mudroom hallway. A drinks table and Sussex chair by Barclay Butera Home offer a restful respite after a day on the ski slopes.

ABOVE: Earth tones impart a warm vibe to a small den that houses a sectional sofa, a pair of Barclay Butera Home Claire storage ottomans, and a view of a breathtaking winter backdrop.

LEFT: A custom painted cabinet depicts a majestic mountain wildlife tableau.

ABOVE: An upholstered leather bed layered with richly patterned bedding and a roomy lounge chair offer an exquisite blend of contemporary luxury with a traditional aesthetic.

FACING ABOVE: The vibrant, energizing colors and patterns used on the draperies and bedding in this small room make it come alive.

BELOW: This narrow but efficient bunk room was designed to accommodate visitors who gravitate to this mountain home for winter fun.

LEFT: This darkly elegant den is a warm sanctuary from the cold winter nights, offering up plenty of places to sit and enjoy the warmth of the fire.

ABOVE: A modern cylinder lamp illuminates the sitting area, while varied textures and earthy tones deliver a relaxed, sophisticated style.

ABOVE LEFT: A cabinet customized with wildlife art delivers a powerful sense of place.

LEFT: Glimmering crystal and pewter-rimmed china adorn a table setting in the dining room.

FACING: Natural elements evoke a woodsy feel, while horns and faux deer heads add to the room's rustic qualities. A tartan plaid rug keeps things warm underfoot.

ABOVE: Chic winter interiors are all about rich, lush materials.

FACING: Leather, linen, and animal prints complement each other very well in this contemporary bedroom.

FACING: Enveloping this bedroom in chocolate brown creates a cocoon-like space. Minimal but stylish furnishings include a woven bed, animal-print Soho cubes, and a chunky wood frame floor mirror.

ABOVE: Woven textures, a natural color palette, and dark woods illustrate the dramatic qualities of a winter woods retreat.

Elegantly appointed, this living room immediately transports the guest to a luxe lodge environment. Hurricane lamps, silver urns, and other decorative items complete the scene in the warmest, most welcoming fashion.

ABOVE: Smart symmetry adds refinement to any space. The winter white palette is set aglow by crystal hurricane lamps and chandeliers. Tufted white upholstery furthers the serene mood.

FACING ABOVE: Beyond the Barclay Butera Home Jacques tufted dining chair against the wall, the dining hall opens onto the living room.

BELOW: The plaid Hudson host chair by Barclay Butera Home adds a dash of pattern and color to the pale palette.

The muted icy hues of an abstract painting reference the tones of a stripped-down winter landscape in this living room tableau.

A plush leather sectional wraps around this visually striking but eminently livable den.

FACING: A velvety brown paint treatment envelops the opulent master bedroom. In the retreat's office, strong, vibrant walls provide the anchor and starting point for the space.

ABOVE: A dramatic, eye-catching sunburst mirror bedazzles a niche off the bedroom.

FACING: The master bath, centered with a freestanding tub, enjoys an unencumbered view of snow-covered mountains.

ABOVE: Contemporary furnishings are fused with patterned fabric and plush textures. Soothing grey-sage walls allow the artwork and remarkable view to pop.

ABOVE: The arrangement of the Barclay Butera Home Lido host chairs and Regency dining chairs introduces clean lines while remaining classic.

RIGHT: A picture-perfect living room showcases the property's dynamic views, no matter if one chooses to perch on the Barclay Butera Home Harbor sofa, Somerset chairs, or the Claire storage ottomans.

ABOVE: Well-chosen furnishings in a palette of muted blues and shades of tan and cream create a low-key, sophisticated environment that echoes the polished mountain vibe of the house.

FACING: An inset fireplace sets off a scheme of beautifully grained marble tile and gives bath time new meaning in this stunning retreat.

ACKNOWLEDGMENTS

A special thanks to:

TAMMY RUS
CHARLES AND KIMBERLY CALDWELL
STEVE AND ANNA EHRLICH
MR. AND MRS. BARKER
MR. .AND MRS. BELJAK
ALLEN AND TAMMY LYDA
MR. AND MR. JULIAN
MR. AND MRS. VILLI
PAT AND ALAN LEWIS
MR. AND MRS. CLOUSE

CALDWELL INTERIOR ARCHITECT/
CYNTHIA CHILDS ARCHITECT, pages 66–79

And thank you to all of my friends
and staff, including:

CHERIE LUNA
CHRISTINE PHILLIPS
SAM AND TIFFANY SLATER
RAY LANG HAMMER
KRISTIN MARIE MORRIS
SAUDI ELVEN
LAUREN KIRSCH
LOIS ICHIKI
JEFF MAYNARD
LAUREL GREEN
JEFF LARSEN
MARIO FERREIRA
STEPHANIE EVANS
DENNIS STOVALL
BIRTE BANT
BRENDON BUTERA
ASHLEY DANG
MEL BORDEAUX

Photography:

MARK LOHMAN, principal photographer
ASHLEY DANG (pages 36, 37, 84 & 85)
LORI BRYSTAN (back cover, page 8)

Barclay Butera has based his career on a passion for beautiful yet livable design. Butera's mantra of redefining luxury has not changed his firm belief in helping his clients achieve the "Better-Best" concept of living. The end result has been a consistent redefinition of home decor luxury and interiors: glamorous and completely approachable. His interior and exterior environments are based upon the philosophy of layering diverse styles of furniture, textiles, and textures. With his licensed partnerships—Kravet Textiles and Carpets, Bradburn Lighting, Eastern Accents Bedding, Merida Natural Fiber Rugs, Mirror Image, Nourison Carpets, and Zodax Home Décor and Fragrance, in addition to the Barclay Butera Lifestyle furniture line (BARCLAYBUTERALIFESTYLE.COM), Butera has made his unique style available to the consumer wanting to add a touch of glamour to their home.

First Edition
17 16 15 14 13   5 4 3 2 1

Text © 2013 Barclay Butera
Photographs © 2013 Mark Lohman and Ashley Dang

Published by
Gibbs Smith
P.O. Box 667
Layton, Utah 84041

1.800.835.4993 orders
www.gibbs-smith.com

Designed by Melissa Dymock
Printed and bound in HongKong

Gibbs Smith books are printed on paper produced from sustainable PEFC-certified forest/controlled wood source. Learn more at www.pefc.org.

LLibrary of Congress Cataloging-in-Publication Data

Butera, Barclay.
Barclay Butera getaways and retreats / Photography by Mark Lohman. — First Edition.
    pages cm
    ISBN 978-1-4236-3300-6
    1. Butera, Barclay—Themes, motives. 2. Interior decoration—United States. 3. Vacation homes—United States. I. Title.
    NK2004.3.B87A4 2013
    747—dc23
    2013008659

BARCLAY BUTERA
SHOWROOMS

BARCLAY BUTERA INTERIORS

WEST HOLLYWOOD
918 North La Cienega Boulevard
West Hollywood, California 90069
TEL 310.432.4252

NEWPORT BEACH
1745 Westcliff Drive
Newport Beach, California 92660
TEL 949.650.8570

PARK CITY
255 Heber Avenue
Park City, Utah 84060
TEL 435.649.5540

WWW.BARCLAYBUTERA.COM